IT'S MIDNIGHT, LORD

IT'S MIDNIGHT, LORD

DOM HELDER CAMARA

Translation by Joseph Gallagher with Thomas Fuller and Tom Conry

ILLUSTRATED BY NAUL OJEDA

THE PASTORAL PRESS

WASHINGTON, D.C.

ISBN 0-912405-02-3

Printed in The United States of America

THE PASTORAL PRESS
225 Sheridan Street, NW
Washington, DC 20011

The Pastoral Press is the publications division of the National Association of
Pastoral Musicians, a membership organization of musicians and clergy dedicated to
fostering the art of musical liturgy.

Book design by Gerard Valerio, Bookmark Studio, Annapolis, Maryland.

Contents

Preface

The poet Sydney Lanier once wrote that "Music is love in search of a word." In the late Seventies the Brazilian Archbishop Dom Helder Camara praised the Swiss Abbé Pierre Kaelin for the music to which he had put some loving words of St. Francis of Assisi. The Abbé thanked him and said that he would be honored to do the same for some of the Archbishop's words.

In the ensuing months, Archbishop Camara — who is the Mother Teresa of Brazil — went in loving pursuit of the words for his vision of the world as it now is and as it might horribly or beautifully become — especially this world as cruelly divided into two worlds: that of the haves and that of the have nots.

Thus was the Symphony of Two Worlds begotten. Camara's searching love for this planet and its diverse peoples had found its words. Kaelin's love had found the music for those words. The Symphony has been performed a number of times in its original French version.

In 1982 Father Virgil Funk, president of the National Association of Pastoral Musicians, resolved to present this Symphony in an English version at the national convention in St. Louis on April 22, 1983. The Archbishop and the Abbé participated in this world English premiere, which 3,000 listeners heard and rapturously applauded.

I had the honor of working on the challenging task of putting the Archbishop's thoughts into English and making the English fit the Abbé's music, which was composed for French sounds and cadences. The English version is now reproduced in this booklet, where it is orchestrated by music for the eye — engravings which poetically match the mood and the themes of the words. Appropriately enough the artist is a member of that Third World in which the Archbishop lives and about which he cares so passionately.

May sympathetic and open-hearted readers put these words and pictures to music by orchestrating their daily lives around the virtues of truth, justice and mercy — virtues which in the Nuclear Age have literally become matters of life and death for this planet and its imperiled populations.

Let this axiom be engraved on every heart: one person can make a difference, and each person should try.

JOSEPH GALLAGHER

IT'S MIDNIGHT, LORD

The text of *It's Midnight, Lord* is adapted from the oratorio for narrator, soloists, choir, and orchestra, entitled **Symphony of Two Worlds**, music by Pierre Kaelin, text by Dom Helder Camara.

The Audacity of the Creator

The audacity of the Creator.

If I had been at Your side, Lord, before You began to create, I would have wanted to help you overcome your reticence. And if the slightest doubt threatened to keep You from creating, I would have spoken up:

> "It's true, Lord, that by making something outside Yourself, You
> will have to forge a broken image. For what You create
> will necessarily reflect You in ways which are multiple,
> finite, bounded, imperfect. But don't hesitate to do it, Lord.
> The courage to create will demonstrate forever Your daring
> and Your humility."

Do it, Lord, You've got to do it now.
You must not doubt; You must strike out;
You must create; enflesh this dream
that You have had since first You dreamed.
Venture forth and fear not most of all
to take Your boldness to its highest heights,
and with it Your lowliness.

Take a tiny pinch of sand
from a tiny planet of dust,
and command man to arise,
man and woman in Your guise,
all creators like Yourself.

Take the risk of humankind,
needful creature spun from clay,
but the one that tames Your heart;
take the risk of humankind,
Your artisan, Your chosen heir.

Great God, only You have power to create.
Come! Use it!

Do it Lord; You've got to do it now;
You must not quail; let hope prevail;
You must create, enflesh the dream
that You have willed since first You dreamed.
Venture forth, and fear not most of all
to take Your boldness to its highest heights,
and with it Your lowliness.

Let Your daring heart dare to go that far;
take risks afresh ev'ry day that dawns;
take risks afresh for eternity;
as children say when fathers leave
to face some test,
"Bon voyage, and best of luck!"

Great God, only You have power to create.
Yes! Do it! Now!

My Sisters and Brothers

Sisters, brothers,
all creation has its eye on us,
is watching.

Each blade, ev'ry tree,
the peachbloom on its stem,
ev'ry star that twins itself
in the mirroring lake;
most of all, all the world
astir with animals.
They stand alert,
poised between their trust and their fear.
All things great and small
surround you ev'rywhere.
A twinge of jealousy,
magnetic wonderment,
compel them to follow your steps,
so alive
so blessed by God.

Sisters and brothers mine,
all God's creation is watching,
has its eye on us,
and feels its doubts arise.

What a sorry mess you've made;
the supreme benefits you have:
a mind that thinks, a chance to choose —
these you employ to hurt yourself.
With these you have betrayed your God.

But the Lord, instead of condemning and crushing us,
shared his liberating presence with us:
the Son of God and the Son of people,
all at once.
Yet we, my brothers and sisters,
what have we made of that life?

Count the cost!
Africa!
Count the cost!
Asia!
Fields of flame and of weeping.
Weigh it!
Latin America riddled with bullets,
hunted down, rounded up.
Where has its music gone?
Where are its carefree songs?
Smothered now underneath cacophony of weapons.
Latin America: outpost remotest of banished hopes;
tortured land of babes leathered by the sun.
Will that sun, flushed with shame,
bury itself,
lose the heart to rise again?
Count the cost!

Soon comes twice one thousand years since He came.
High mounts the debt before us.
Weigh it! The sum is dreadful!

Count the cost!
See the poor waste away
in the midst of wasteful nations.
See the cost!
The ones who bear the most:
the pariahs of needy nations.

They scream at you.
They cannot understand.
They scream at you.
They cannot understand.
Can you still turn away,
so frightened of what they say?

Sisters, brothers,
all creation sounds a warning:
hear its siren.

Soon comes twice one thousand years since He came.
Crushing, the debt we shoulder.
Weigh it!
The heft is fearsome!

which self will win?

You are well aware, my brothers and sisters,
that we are sufficiently feeble to trigger off
the third and final world war,
and to use our monstrously sorrowful power
to erase all life from the face of the earth.
You know as well that we are sufficiently strong
to wipe away from the same earth
ever more of its misery,
especially political oppression.

At first glance, it seems that hatred has conquered the earth.
Since the end of the Second World War
how many local wars have erupted!
The nations that manufacture weapons,
how they have multiplied.
And how the arms race has made these weapons
ever more sophisticated and disastrous.
Countries which lack essentials for their people
have not hesitated to plunge themselves
into hopeless debt in order to appease
the goddess of national security.
Because of this waste, in countries everywhere,
whatever their political creed,
there are kidnappings,
torture, murders,
people who disappear,
never to be seen again;
exiles, refugees.
And behind all this terror and insecurity
hides the consumer society.

Who will lift this woeful weight,
all these crushing concerns of state?
How they choke the breath from countless
children of God!

Who will lift away
these burdens which wind up killing
more than the bloodiest war?

Who will lift this woeful weight,
all these grievous concerns of state?
How they squeeze the life from countless
children of God.

Which self will win,
the strong or the feeble?
Which will prevail?

I know them both so well:
the feeble self is mine.
Its matricidal might to kill my parent planet.
I need but start the war
that will surely be the last one,
a mushroom coffin for the gifts entrusted me.

Yes, I should know them both:
The better self is mine.
I know I'm strong enough to mend this fractured planet,
to break the chains that shackle,
to end the rage of hunger,
to feed the sense of justice that has been given me.

Behold before you now all the rivers of hate;
they swell on ev'ry side
and portend a deadly fate.
Behold around you now
how nations race to arm;
while military helmets
obscure doom's last alarm.

Their state security
is a goddess much adored;
for her they stab their people
with old and rusty swords.
They call it public safety;
they torture, they expel.
Beneath the cry of order!
all freedoms hear their knell.

.ojeda

Behold around you now
tyrant states and wasted wealth.
They even waste the future
with their monetary stealth.
Behold around you now
all this wretchedness and rage,
inhuman situations,
but who can save the age?

Which self will win,
the strong or the feeble?
Which will prevail?

The Spirit is Breathing

The spirit is breathing.

All those with eyes to see,
women and men with ears for hearing
detect a coming dawn;
a reason to go on.

They seem small, these signs of dawn,
perhaps ridiculous.

All those with eyes to see,
women and men with ears for hearing
uncover in the night
a certain gleam of light;
they see the reason to go on.

For when God stands at David's side,
Goliath suddenly is small.
When God's grace fortifies the frail, the giants tremble and fall.

How else explain this unexpected marvel?
The weak feel suddenly new strength,
the will to fight their bondage,
without the need of going mad,
of placing hope in hopeless bombs.
Such defense these souls will never choose.
Only tyrants worship monster bombs.
Let them keep such a god,
doomsday god,
lord of all who play with suicide.

All those with eyes to see,
women and men with ears for hearing
discover all the while
these hints of hope are growing.
All those with eyes to see,
women and men with ears for hearing
have found without a doubt sure signs of hope;
they clasp them close, these signs of hope,
cure for hopelessness.

The weak discover that they can make themselves
strong and invincible by uniting — uniting not to attack
others, but to defend themselves and their rights
as human beings. For those rights do not arise from
political power, nor from mere military strength, but
are the gift of the Creator.

These foundational rights of man, woman and child;
they are not grudging gifts from the ruling class,
nor from the strong.
These rights under all rights of man, woman and child:
they are the gifts of God above,
a rooted gift that is our birthright,
bred in our bloodstream.

How else can you explain the birth of numberless
humanitarian movements in rich, industrial lands —
movements with different methods, but all with one
common goal: the determination to help create a
world more livable, more just and more humane.

Holy breathing of God,
I feel You stirring.

Warmed by this breath good things start to grow.
Even in strong, wealthy lands
fresh, mobilizing calls evoke planetary piety,
winning the hearts and the hands of the caring:
each in her chosen path,
each with his special gift,
take their stand
to create a world more fit for living,
more just and more humane.

You whisper a lesson of strength
to all people joined together,
and gather the hopeful legions of the poor.
You want them to learn how to join
with the armies of justice,
aroused in wealthy lands from richly caring hearts.
May they both fashion soon
a world more fit for living,
more just and more humane.

Holy breathing of God,
I hear You whisper.
Your Spirit sighs:
"My love is stronger than hatred."
It sighs:
"My love will vanquish hatred."

The Spiral of Violence

And in those days . . .

Children were bragging,
full of creative imagination.

My dad has a motorboat.
Mine has the fastest yacht afloat.
Our dad has a shore
with cruisers by the score.

Tra la la . . .

My mom has a Cadillac
with a TV in the back.
What a tacky choice;
come see our new Rolls Royce.

Tra la la . . .

My dad has a great big jet;
no one ever beat him yet.
Our dad has him beat;
he just acquired a fleet.

I have just a single grip
ready for my trip to far away.
To where?
Just check the news one day soon:
My mom and I, we're flying to the moon,
to the moon, yes, some day soon.

A nd in those days . . .

Childish people were boasting,
full of destructive madness.

Thank me, the one who set it ablaze:
World War One —
Verdun and all the highways to death,
one by one.
First class war,
war without peer,
a carnival.

Your grimy Great War! Hah!
Child's play compared to mine.
Thank me, the one who set it ablaze:
World War Two —
Auschwitz and all the speedways to death,
two by two.
Human nature,
fallen face down:
Hiroshima!

Fabulous entertainment,
just like some neat holiday fireworks:
Hiroshima!

Get me! I could really unleash it:
World War Three —
My war would surely merit the name:
Last World War.
I possess now
ten times over
all that is needful
to make an end of life here,
all life on God's green earth.
Adieu, adieu, adieu good mother earth.

And in those days . . .

Meantime, the Third World was wondering in silence:

And what of us?

Bowed beneath our miseries,
have we not the worst war,
have we not the harshest of wars?

Ev'ry day our agonies,
filling up our graveyards,
killing more than both of your Great Wars.

Make no mistake, my sisters and brothers:
The beginning of violence is misery —
misery that poisons housing, jobs,
diversions, health, life itself —
all that oppresses and exploits.

All this killing,
all this crying,
what's the diff'rence
if all are dying?
This is warfare —
some die slow,
hungry and homeless,
alone.

When poverty erupts it brings violence on a new scale:
attacks, robberies, assassinations, loathings.
When poverty explodes it shatters smug security
and leaves a hunger for vengeance.

All our wanting,
it wreaks its vengeance;
all our anguish,
it rents its fury;
all our weeping,
pain unsleeping —
these give birth to our rages.

Finally comes repression,
and the institutionalization of violence —
repression so often savage and brutal.
Already we are in the full spiral of violence.

How it spirals,
all that violence,
If you would fight it,
all that violence,
you first must fight
all that privation.
That's the true war —
all that oppression.

And us, what of us,
all the children of this earth?
Tomorrow comes;
our day will dawn.
Two thousand years since that Child.
Think of that,
even today.

In the Middle of the Night

In the middle of the night.
When stark night was darkest,
then You chose to come.

God's resplendent first-born
sent to make us one.

The voices of doom protest:
"All these words about justice,
love and peace —
all these naive words
will buckle beneath the weight of a reality
which is brutal and bitter, ever more bitter."
It is true, Lord, it is midnight upon the earth,
moonless night and starved of stars.
But can we forget that You,
the Son of God,
chose to be born precisely at midnight?

If you had been afraid of shadows
You would have been born at noon.
But you preferred the night.

Lord, you were born in the middle of the night
because midnight is pregnant with dawn.

When midnight casts its spell
ev'ry hope is like old dried-up ink
in the bottom of a well.
When darkness cloaks the night
I come naked to the gates of hope;
all the locks are bolted tight.
The blacker the night
the farther off seems the dawn;
the past infects the night
and not yet stir the rays of today.

When slowest drags the dark
and the flock of frightened shadows rove,
list'ning vainly for the lark.
When phantoms wander wild,
I go out and take my orphan place
With each cold, defrauded child.

The blacker the night
the farther off seems the dawn;
the past infects the night
and not yet glows the gift of today.

Entrapped in pitchy night,
from the deeps of all my shadows
I have seen the gloom ignite;
louder far than throats of mourning
cries an infant voice aborning.

The darker the night,
the more joyful the dawn;
the deadly past is dead
when the sun is reborn —
precious present, gift of now.

And you, Woman, you have heard in the night
that cry of a newborn.
But the imperial ones, they did not understand.
Those kingdoms of yesteryear,
where are they now?

But the pessimists cry out again:
"Today those empires have been surpassed.
Even the superpowers have been overtaken
by apocalyptic, multi-national alliances
that control economics and military power,
the cleverest minds and the most influential media."

The pessimists continue:
"Often enough, in the face of such conspiracies
even the forces of religion fall into the gears."

"Such cartels mock political systems.
They have dug in and made themselves at home
from north to south,
from east to west."
It's true, Lord,
it is the deepest midnight.

But how can we forget
that the darker is the night,
the lovelier dawn.

And us, what 'of us?
Don't your children fill your minds?
Soon enough we must take your place,
for the year Two Thousand beckons us.

O Dawn! After such a dark!
Will you see two worlds now joined as one?
One song?
One great symphony?

Two worlds that beat as one!

One song!

Which self will win, my sisters and my brothers?
Feel God's holy breathing in the middle of the night!

Two worlds!
Just one symphony!